The World According to
BAXTER BLACK
Quips, Quirks and Quotes

CANIS LaTeRaNS
UNQULaTe OVerPeYSON CO.

All poems written by Baxter Black
Copyright © 2008 by Baxter Black

Published by: Coyote Cowboy Company
PO Box 2190
Benson, AZ 85602

Cover and book design by Becky Harvey

LIBRARY OF CONGRESS CATALOGING IN PUBLICATION DATA
Main entry under:
Cowboy Poetry

Bibliography: p
1. World According to Baxter Black Quips, Quirks, & Quotes
2. Cowboy-Poetry
3. Poetry-Cowboy
4. Humor-Cowboy
5. Agriculture-Poetic Comment

I. Black, Baxter, 1945-

Library of Congress # 2008905491
ISBN-13: 978-0-939343-52-2
ISBN-10: 0-939343-52-5

OTHER BOOKS BY BAXTER
The Cowboy and His Dog
A Rider, A Roper And A Heck'uva Windmill Man
On The Edge Of Common Sense, The Best So Far
Doc, While Yer Here
Buckaroo History
Coyote Cowboy Poetry
Croutons On A Cow Pie
The Buckskin Mare
Cowboy Standard Time
Croutons On A Cow Pie, Vol 2
Hey, Cowboy, Wanna Get Lucky? *(Crown Publishing, Inc.)*
Dunny And The Duck
Cow Attack
Cactus Tracks And Cowboy Philosophy *(Crown Publishing, Inc.)*
A Cowful Of Cowboy Poetry
Horseshoes, Cowsocks And Duckfeet *(Crown Publishing, Inc.)*
Ag Man The Comic Book
Hey, Cowgirl, Need A Ride? *(Crown Publishing, Inc.)*
Blazin' Bloats & Cows On Fire!

baxterblack.com

TABLE OF CONTENTS

INTRODUCTION

INTRODUCTION

This book is a refresher course in the wit and wisdom, the fun and folly, the grin and the grit of Baxter Black, cowboy poet.

It displays the carefully crafted nonsense, the rabidinous rhymes, multiparous metaphors and the strangled similes that pepper his work like . . . like . . . croutons on a cowpie!

Where letters co-mingle, dangle and jingle
Like drops on the tip of a nose
And words conflagrate, ignoring their fate
Throwing sparks that sprinkle the prose

In a tinnious blur like the rowel of a spur
Spinning loops from the web of his mind
It's poem synthesis, though others insist
It comes from a spider's behind!

C🤠wboy Mentality

ON COWBOY WEDDINGS

The bride was lovely. She stood out like a penguin in a patch of Sandhill cranes. The groom's party looked like they were still on hangers.

When the father of the bride was called upon to answer, 'who gives this woman to be wed,' Raymond said, "Her mother and I...and the Valley Bank, I guess."

At the bride's request we played "Walkin' the Dog" as the wedding party marched out. It was fitting, I guess, because Billy's ol' dog Bronc caught the bouquet!

AFTERTHOUGHT
Nuptiphobia - fear of catchin' the corsage.

ON FINDING A SPUR

I came to a low water crossing
where the trails converged near the bank
All by itself I spotted a spur
that lay buried plum up to the shank.

I kicked at the dirt all around it
but its mate was not to be found
Then I wondered just what circumstances
had led to the spur in the ground.

I finally unraveled the mystery.
My answer was there in the sands
The tracks of his horse went round in a circle.
The spur was a one leg-ged man's!

AFTERTHOUGHT

After Uncle Leonard had his leg amputated below the knee he recovered quickly, wore the prosthesis and was soon walking. "Pretty good," I told him. "Yup," he said, "I'm not doin' bad for a guy with one foot in the grave."

ON BEIN' A COWBOY

It ain't easy bein' a cowboy
so I've made myself a vow.
To avoid inspection and public rejection I'll
just stay out here with the cows.
'Cause if it was easy, I'd be somethin' else.

AFTERTHOUGHT

The cowboy mentality can best be demonstrated by this little joke. Hold your hand up in front of your face, about two inches from palm to nose and repeat after me, "Bet ya can't hit my hand before I move it!"

ON JUST SAYING 'NO'!

"I know Carter took her out but she's not that kind of a girl."

JUST SAY NO!

"No, I've never heard a horse bark like that before either, but I don't think it's serious."

JUST SAY NO!

"The Indians ate this part right after they killed the buffalo."

JUST SAY NO!

"If you elect me," **JUST SAY**..well, you know.

AFTERTHOUGHT

Resistance to temptation is the true measure of character.
- Unknown

ON ALL OR NOTHING

I admit I was once an ALL OR NOTHING personality. It's a cross many bear unconsciously. I've tried to keep my enthusiasm in check so I can be better company for those around me, but it's hard to see both sides when you've got one eye closed. Matter of fact, the one thing I couldn't do in excess...was moderation.

AFTERTHOUGHT
To truly understand me you need to know when to listen to me and when not to.

ON STUPID QUESTIONS

I've never seen a horse do a complete back flip. Did you teach him that?

This Elko is quite a place. Which one of you guys is a cowboy poet?

That's a great tattoo. Were you drunk?

Sure I can run one of these things! How do you start it?

Fifty dollars on a pair of threes! Were you bluffing?

Were you scared? Better go back to the house and change.

AFTERTHOUGHT
He bucked clean outta the saddle
so high that his bad breath condensed
And come down a'cussin' and lighted
a'straddle a dang bob wire fence.

It cut him right up to the buckle
between his feet and his chin
He just let his stirrups out longer
and rode his ol' pony on in!

ON STEPPING OUTSIDE THE RV TRAILER FOR A QUICK WHIZ WITHOUT NOTIFYING THE DRIVER

He heard the crunch of gravel. In his desperate lunge, he almost caught the aluminum awning strut on the back of the camper, but he stepped on a bottle cap and skittered sideways like a bad billiards shot.

He stood alongside the road as his wife accelerated from the intersection, sore-footed, white, embarrassed and hatless in his threadbare, holey Fruit of the Looms with the frayed elastic and baggy seat. He looked like Cupid gone to seed.

AFTERTHOUGHT
His underwear looked like a pirate ship flag under attack!

Wanted: Cowboy. No TV. No phone. If you don't like dogs and can't tough it in the mountains don't apply. -Alamo, NV

ଛଔଓଃ

When in Rome wear your cowboy boots.

There's two things a cowboy's afraid of: bein' stranded afoot, and a decent woman.

First thing I ask a cowboy when he tells me he's getting married is, "Does she have a job?"

I quit wearing fringed loincloths, they get caught in my zipper.

ଛଔଓଃ

There's lots of cowboys out there, friends, you just can't see 'em from the road!

ON COWBOY POETRY GATHERINGS

But with so many cowboy poets
and so many stories to tell
   Not every poem that we'd ever
     written got told, though we
       tried, to beat hell.

   Part of the problem, I reckon,
 was time, and therein good
   friends, was the pinch
 'Cause we'd each planned to
   disclose a mile of prose and was
   asked to recite just an inch!

AFTERTHOUGHT

I tried to explain cowboy poetry to a television crew in Nashville. They looked at me like I had toilet paper stuck to my shoe and sent me after coffee.

ON SPENDING THE CATTLE CHECK

This particular fall Oley did well with his cattle sale. After paying his taxes he hit the bar. He was welcome as formaldehyde at a footrot party!

He celebrated! Rising and reciting, philosophizing and falling, partying and passing out! Standing to deliver, holding his own. Wringing every ounce of feeling from the wash rag of life. Reaching the queasy edges of sickness and sanity, round the corners of delirium, riding the roller coaster of incontinence! But a man can only have so much fun.

AFTERTHOUGHT

When he appeared at the dining room toweled and fresh he looked like a pink cockleburr. Half way home Oley got to tuggin' at his collar, complaining that his longjohns were chokin' him! He peeled off his shirt and dropped his britches, straining and grunting like a moulting lobster. "No wonder, yer stranglin'," said his pardner, "You've got yer longjohns on upside down!"

ON TAKING HARD CLASSES IN SCHOOL

Looming ahead of me was two semesters of Organic Chemistry, two semesters of Physics and one five hour course in Calculus and Triggernometry. I felt like Gutzon Borglum standing in front of Mt. Rushmore with a plastic spoon.

AFTERTHOUGHT

I had the highest temperature in my class.

ON HANGIN' OUT

Hangin' out is an art. There is a fine line between hangin' out and goofing off (Note: when teenagers do it, it is always 'goofing off.') Pinto applied for a job at the feedlot as an EXPERT. He told them he'd put in so much 'hang time' he'd accumulated more knowledge than most.

I asked him how he made out. "I think the boss was a pretty good judge of character," he said, "He didn't hire me."

AFTERTHOUGHT
I'm not an actor but I play one on TV.

ON DUNNY AND THE DUCK

Young Orville hefted up a duck which kinda
    starts this caper
  Behind unfazed, ol' Dunny raised his tail
    to break a vapor.

Why people do the things they do remains a
    constant wonder
  Like Orville there, saw tail mid-air, and
    stuck the duck up under!

Ol' Dunny rared and broke his reins! The
    other horses bolted
  And ran askew while feathers flew like
    Pegasus had moulted!

AFTERTHOUGHT

The best way to describe the relationship between the cowboy and his blue heeler, it's sort of a 'hike it to me and go out for a pass!'

Gallimaufry

ON GOLF

I was teamed up with a professional at a celebrity golf tournament. He asked me how I played. I said, "Not too well." I'm sure he thought I was being modest, because after the first hole he turned to me and said, "You really DON'T play too well, do ya?"

By the third hole we'd traded our golf cart in on an all-terrain vehicle and the rest of our foursome was driving an armored personnel carrier. A nice feller lent me his golf bag and a pocket full of balls. I lost them all. I was ashamed to tell him. I lost so many balls that we eventually rented a backhoe for the sand trap and hired two scuba drivers to join our caravan.

AFTERTHOUGHT
The only good ball I hit was when I stepped on the sand rake!

ON FEELING MUTUAL

I ran into a couple on the London streets at midnight. His hair was sticking up on top and straight out along the edges. The fringe was dyed fluorescent orange and the vertical portion dyed fluorescent yellow. He looked like a cross between a Russian Thistle and a highway flare. I figgered someone set it on fire and put it out with a weed eater!

I stopped him and asked If I could take his picture. He said, "I was jus' tellin' me bird the same thing!"

AFTERTHOUGHT
It took us eight hours to fly from London to Minneapolis. Such a short time. Makes you wonder why they didn't discover us sooner?

ON THE ENGLISH DIET

The English have never tried to conquer the world with their culinary prowess. I regret I couldn't drink the Guiness ale. It reminded me of that black fluid that runs out of the low end of a silage pit.

While we were at the auction market in Skipton, in the Yorkshire Dales of England we struck up a conversation with Mr. Morris Smith, age 77. He milked ten head of cows and ran a flock of ewes. He asked where we were from. We said we'd come up from London on the train. "London," he said thoughtfully, "Neva been m'self. Neva saw the point."

AFTERTHOUGHT

Curiosity. Sheep have it. Cats, kids, antelopes, even auctioneers have it. It has nothing to do with intelligence.

ON SAM'S CHICKENS

Sam raises chickens. Not in a big way, but chickens are like CDs or DVDs, if you're gonna have one, you might as well have a bunch.

One day I helped him make a run to the chicken sale at Mai Van's Oriental Grocery and Unusual Seafood. We gathered up all the old hens in the neighborhood, plus a few grasshopper ducks and loaded them in the back of his pickup. Down the road we went with our convoy of foundering feathered fossils trailing duck down and chicken fluff like a cattail in the hands of a three year old!

We netted $27 after gas and beer. Not bad for a day's wok.

AFTERTHOUGHT

I walked into Dee's Lounge and Feed Store in south Louisiana. The sign on the door said COLD BEER AND BABY CHICKS TO GO.

IN DEFENSE OF THE CHICKEN

Some say this ignoble creature
with his intellect unrefined
And lack of civilized manners
has little to offer mankind

But let me suggest the chicken
had two contributions to make.
The first was the peckin' order,
the second, the chicken fried steak!

AFTERTHOUGHT

I eat every egg I can. It's one less chicken I have to contend with!

ON REHEATED CHILI AND BEANS

Breakfast was an unpleasant déjà vu. The reheated chili and beans was the consistency of South Dakota gumbo and smelled like burning brakes. For supper we had chili and bean sludge. It was the closest I'd come to eating lava. That night we slept outside!

AFTERTHOUGHT

Breakfast is the most important meal of the day...if you ain't home by then, boy, yer in real trouble!

25

ON LIFE CHOICES

The newspaper photo showed them leaning into the harmony like four caroling coyotes! I'm glad I didn't try to make a living singing.

Today I'd probably belong to a group that hadn't named themselves yet. One seeking a new identity at every engagement. A side man at the Trailer Court Christmas Concerto, strummin' rhythm guitar with Pinto and the Play for Food Band.

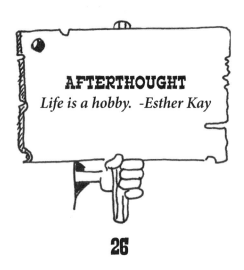

AFTERTHOUGHT
Life is a hobby. -Esther Kay

ON CONCERTS

When my daughter was a teen she was dreamy over mall music. Sort of a semi solid margarine rock and roll. Then she discovered ACID ROCK! I took her to a live concert of a big star. She loved it. I was thankful that I had taken earplugs.

The closest I'd ever been to one of those concerts was the Indianapolis 500! Between the spectacular light show and the screaming teenagers it was like a cross between Cape Canaveral and castrating pigs in a metal building!

AFTERTHOUGHT
She saw the light, and joined the dark side. - Darth Vader

ON THE BARR LAKE INN

Jim says you walk up to the door and there's a sign on it that says USE OTHER DOOR. You walk around to the other door. There's a sign on it that says WATCH YER STEP, and there ain't no step!

AFTERTHOUGHT

Eleven pm, elbow deep in bar flies, beer drying in your lap, seven dollars wadded up in yer shirt pocket and hope in your heart. If you've been there, this song is dedicated to you!

ON THINKIN' TWICE ABOUT STARTING SOMETHING

There in the hole, like a power pole stood the pressure for all of his peers, UGLY FOR HIRE, and he wore a truck tire that come down over his ears. He had on some chaps with big rubber straps but over his arms instead and sported a pattern like the planet Saturn, his eyebrows went clear round his head!

His good eye glared while his nostrils flared like a winded Lippizan. Which lent him the air of a wounded bear whose pointer'd been stepped upon. A crescent wrench swung from where it hung on a log chain wrapped 'round his neck, along with a claw, a circular saw, and parts from a Harley wreck.

With his Sumo girt, he needed no shirt, Heck, he had no place to tuck it. And wonders don't cease, he wore a cod piece made from a back-hoe bucket!

AFTERTHOUGHT
Some people take up too much space in a small room.

ON BAD LUCK

He is one of those fellers that is plagued by the angel of Bad Luck, Saint Misfortune. Gremlins followed him around dropping rocks on his toes, slipping ropes underneath his horse's tail, and laying banana peels in his path.

He reached up and grabbed the wire. "What the heck is this doin' up here!" He pulled on it a couple times like he was trying to stop a train. He jerked. The 20 penny nail holding it to the wall came free, whirled around like a bullwhip and went right through his upper lip.

I heard him cry. It was not the first time. He was standing frozen on the floor. The nail quivered in place and the wire hummed like a dial tone.

AFTERTHOUGHT

How was the game? They kicked a field goal on the kick-off and we missed the extra point.

People don't "own" mules anymore than they "own" cats. They are both just living at your place and doing as little as they can to stay there.

Donnaisms - Donna Goiri:
- "How's your drink?" "I don't know . . . I can't tell until I get sick."
- "Are we married or did you not hear me?"

I've just been sittin' around gettin' on my own nerves. - Pinto

---

He hadn't had a haircut since his sister's wedding and his beard looked like the ground side of a bale of hay.

My brand new pickup had it's left hind cocked up on a jack like a dog markin' his territory.

ON BIRD HUNTING

Wes was an experienced bird hunter. He bagged a pheasant, a grouse and a prairie chicken. I was impressed. He said, "Now if I can just git a medda lark, I'll have a Minnesota Grand Slam!

I asked how medda lark tasted. "Oh," he said, "bout like a owl."

AFTERTHOUGHT

They say you are what you eat. I say, you are what you step in.

32

ON FRUITLESS HUNTING TRIPS

Lo, the weary hunter came,
no blood upon his hands.
His darlin' wife, in sweet relief,
bid welcome to her man.

She bore his epic saga as wives are
forced to bear. But winced when
he said she forgot to pack his
underwear.

She stilled the mighty hunter,
her answer left him stunned
"You must have overlooked
them, Dear, I packed them
with your gun."

AFTERTHOUGHT

I went into a bar and ordered a Martinez. The bartender said, "You mean martini?" "No," I said, "I can only drink one."

ON ROADKILL COATS

It's the wisdom of Solomon's voice...
the perfect solution, it grants absolution,
yet leaves the owner Pro Choice!

Make it a habit to pick up your rabbit,
Don't leave him to dry in the sun.
For the sake of a garment,
recycle your varmint,
it's tacky to just hit and run!

AFTERTHOUGHT
Cars don't run over cats . . . people do. Ban People!

Veterinarians

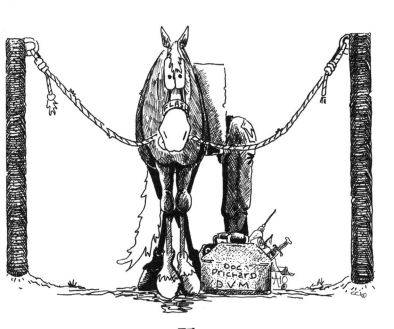

ON CATS

I had a lady ask me what it meant when a cat starts tearin' up the upholstery, sharpens his claws on the Lazy Boy, and all the hair falls off his tail. I said, "Ma'am, that means it's time to get a new cat!"

AFTERTHOUGHT

To paraphrase Elmer Kelton who said, "There is no dishonor in farming as long as you don't take money for it." I say, "There is no dishonor in small animal veterinary practice as long as you don't take money for it."

ON VETERINARY TELEPHONE ETIQUETTE

Rule #1 - Never speak directly to a client. Make them describe all the symptoms to a secretary, a wife, the kennel boy or the drug salesman who happens to be in the office at the time.

Many clients retaliate by having their wife, six year old, or hired man make the call in the first place!

AFTERTHOUGHT

Veterinarians don't wear a tie to work. They approach their business like a professional football player, knowing when the game's over they're gonna look a lot worse.

ON THE VETERINARIAN SPOUSE'S LAUNDRY

The vet'inary's laundry
can disrupt a married life.
It's enough to make you jealous
of a truck mechanic's wife.

But there is no lofty moral,
just a sense of déjà vu,
A warning now remembered,
that should have been a clue.

When your spouse gave you their hanky
as your darlin'-one-to-be,
You should have been suspicious
when it smelled like tomcat pee!

AFTERTHOUGHT

The doctor had not realized that his surgical assistant had used flammable ether during the surgery when he used the electrocautry to stop a bleeder on a freshly spayed cat. He was later heard to comment, "It's hard to blow out a Persian!" - Dr. T.S.

ON PHILOSOPHICAL MYSTERIES

Does horseradish make fishes' eyes water, and why do dogs roll in fresh cow manure?

I do know this, be careful letting a dog lick your face, for the same reason you should hesitate before shaking a veterinarian's hand . . . you never know where it's been!

AFTERTHOUGHT

If one becomes a philosopher by getting a degree in philosophy, what do you call someone with a degree in parasitology . . . ?

ON PESTILENCE

Ticks the size of Tootsie Pops
transfuse a cow a day
And two can pack a yearlin' off
or pull a one-horse sleigh.

We tell ourselves God gave us brains
to halt their ill effect
And though He made all living things,
He gave us intellect

So how come we can't beat those bugs?
Methinks we've too much pride.
Though God made us, remember
He ain't always on our side!

AFTERTHOUGHT

I don't think that would make a good poem but it's free versable.

ON RESTRAINT OF LARGE ANIMALS

Porphus illadees. From the Latin, Porphus: meaning 'livestock handling or holding equipment' and illadees: meaning 'last repaired in 1986.'

AFTERTHOUGHT
There is no foolproof way of restraining livestock save shooting them from a distance then sending your brother-in-law in to check for a pulse.

41

ON VETERINARIANS VS NUTRITIONISTS

Called to the feedlot during an emergency, the consulting nutritionist arrived, drove to the pen and rolled down his power window. He counted the necropsied carcasses and remarked to the busy, occupied veterinarian, "Do you think after cuttin' up six you're convinced it's bloat?"

Dr. Miles waved the flies away and answered, "You wanna post the other six to see for yourself?"

The nutritionist studied him a minute, powered up his window and drove off.

Doc turned to the cowboy helpin' him and said, "Ya know, when they invented electric windows they reduced the nutritionist's work load by 50%."

AFTERTHOUGHT
The cause of most airplane accidents is, "The pilot does everything wrong too fast, and everything right too slow!"--Steve Wilson

ON ROPING VETERINARIANS

Dr. Huey, DVM, went out to look at a tobacco farmer's sick calf. "He's in the pasture, Doc. I'm too busy but yer young... you can catch him!"

Doc drug his rope out from behind the seat of his vet truck and started swingin' it. He knocked the old man's hat off before it finally hung up on the side mirror of the pickup.

"You aren't very good at that, are ya?" asked the old man suspiciously.

"Not too, but it don't make any difference," says Doc, "I charge a dollar a throw whether I catch'em or not!"

The old man yelled over his shoulder, "Leroy, git out there and catch that calf for the good doctor!"

AFTERTHOUGHT
A cowman is as good as a cowboy, til you need a cowboy.

ON COUNTRY VETERINARIANS

Why just last week two farmers were talkin'
outside my clinic door
"Doc ain't perfect, but for our little town you
couldn't ask for more."

"Yeah, I'll agree," the second one said,
"I've given it some thought
With Doc, you always get your money's
worth...but he don't charge a lot."

AFTERTHOUGHT

*It's not how much you make, it's, did they get their
money's worth.*

ON BEIN' LOST

Harold was boss of the truckers.
I figgered he might set me right.
So I called him up on the two way
and explained my desperate plight.

He said, "Describe your surroundings."
I looked for a landmark somewhere.
"Ain't nothin' but rocks and sagebrush."
He said, "Sonny, yer almost there!"

AFTERTHOUGHT
Darden said the further he chased her the dimmer she grew.

Cows

ON EXOTIC BREEDING

To improve his herd's efficiency Mr. Boards found some ampules of kangaroo semen. They worked great but he couldn't keep the cross-breds in the corral. He later attempted to incorporate some grizzly bear in his herd's blood lines by using artificial insemination. He was in the hospital when I called to see how it worked. Apparently he had encountered some problems during the collection process.

AFTERTHOUGHT

I explained to Willie that my son was having disciplinary problems in school. He said, "Well, you just can't swim outside the gene pool."

ON ARDEL'S COWS

Now Ardel's cows were all crossbred,
in the fullest sense of the word
Part hippo, Holstein or llama,
and prob'ly some Yak in the herd

He had one ol' Braymer confusion
whose hide was as loose as a goose
With a hump that flapped like a diaper
and pendulous lips like a moose.

AFTERTHOUGHT
*One of the greatest feelings in the world is to see a cow
loose on the highway . . . and realize it's not yours!*

ON BOVINE BEAUTY

". . . the cow was ugly as the linoleum under your refrigerator. Evolution took one look at her and said, "This is where we take a fork in the road! I believe she has the brain stem of a tuber.""

AFTERTHOUGHT

There was a healed lump at the angle of her jaw, her left horn curled back into the side of her head, and the right horn swooped out gracefully to the northeast. She looked like she was directing traffic!

ON EXCUSES TO KEEP AN OLD COW THAT NEEDS TO BE CULLED

She'll be good as new once the hair grows back.

My sister-in-law had a C-section and we didn't ship her.

You can't cull one just because she can't walk as fast as the others.

I know she's barren, but look how fat she is.

I say as long as three outta four works, she's worth keepin'.

If she had Brucellosis, I'd know it!

That's not lump jaw. She's only got misaligned nostrils.

AFTERTHOUGHT

Fine replacement, bred and pregged. Pay no mind to that bad leg, she's a dandy, not too old . . . tit's'll grow back so I'm told.

ON COW CALCULATIONS

Harold justified buying a new pickup every year or two using a mathematical formula determined by figgering how many cows it took to buy a new vehicle.

Twenty years ago, he explained it took 35 cows at $250 each to buy an $8,000 pickup. This year it takes 20 cows at $800 each to buy a $16,000 pickup.

According to his calculations, the way pickups are goin' down in price, how could he afford not to trade!

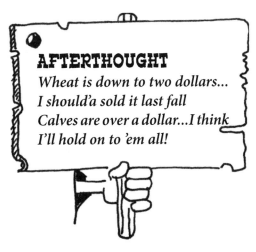

AFTERTHOUGHT
Wheat is down to two dollars...
I should'a sold it last fall
Calves are over a dollar...I think
I'll hold on to 'em all!

ON THE MARKET

A genius, he humbly admits to himself, smart as a tree full of owls.

Twenty foot tall with a bulletproof brain, a friend to all of his pals.

So just like the story of Jekyll and Hyde he's a wise man or a clown.

A hero or fool depending on whether the market goes up or goes down!

AFTERTHOUGHT

"The only cattle making money today," said the old rancher, "are those raised in the shade...the shade of an oil well!"

ON THE LETTER TO THE BANKER

Enclosed is a check for the live ones, sold
every cow we could find
I'm sending a detailed accounting forthwith,
to try and settle your mind.

There's still two at large in the cedars, not
much just a couple of snides
If we can't get'em caught by Friday, we'll
shoot'em and bring in the hides!

AFTERTHOUGHT
*Banks have one very special advantage that most other
special interest groups don't have. They have the most
powerful lobby group in the country . . . the Federal
Reserve Board.*

ON IMPROVISING CALF PULLERS

On the instruction of his father-in-law, Terry soon had the yellow plastic ski rope attached to the calf's legs. The remainder of the poly line lay coiled ominously behind him. It snarled and gaped like a rhino trap. Shurnuf, a wreck ensued!

Down the other side of the swell they sailed, Terry tangled in the line and tobogganing like a 200 pound ham tied to a runaway buffalo! Through the brush and rock they careened until the calf popped out and Terry plowed to a stop.

Finally he stood at an angle emptying 20 pounds of New Mexico soil out of his boxer shorts. He pointed out the danger in his father-in-law's plan. How he'd narrowly escaped being killed.

"Well," said Dad, "Heifers that good are hard to come by and you're just my... well, heifers that good are hard to come by."

AFTERTHOUGHT
Tom and Leroy had the perfect arrangement: Nobody else would work for Leroy and nobody else would hire Tom.

ON THE FETAL EYE VIEW

Say, anybody got a light?
It sure is dark in here
And tighter than the skin on Polish sausage.

For nine long months I've trusted Mom but
now she's pulled the plug!
A pure and simple case of double crossage.

AFTERTHOUGHT

*Calving involves a lot more than simply inserting a coin,
punching a button, and watching a can of Diet Coke be
born with a thunk!*

ON LONGHORN CATTLE

The popularity of Longhorn cattle in modern times stems from a sense of tradition. After all, the Jersey breed can claim the same calving ease advantage but how many ranchers do you know that would keep 38 head of purebred Jerseys between the house and the road?

AFTERTHOUGHT

Listenin' to them purebred folks makes me think right now New Delhi's not the only place they have a sacred cow.

ON COW CHIP COOKING

There's something that strikes me as ironic,
that borders on being abuse.

It's cooking steaks on a cow chip fire...Like
stewing you in your own juice.

There are chips of all kinds in abundance from
poker to micro to munk,

Yet the cow stands alone as a victim to be
fricasseed over a punk!

AFTERTHOUGHT
I eat beef - - I eat it to get even.

ON ROPING A COW
OVER THE FENCE

I'll spare the gruesome details
'cause you've heard'em all before
Every cowboy's been a victim
in this kind of tug-a-war

Bein' caught between a buckin' horse
who's finally jumped the fence
And a pig-eyed cow who stood her ground
in sullen self-defense

AFTERTHOUGHT
She'll kick when she can and smash his ol' fingers and never make him a dime. Tear down the corral, get choked in the chute and go out the wrong gate every time!

ON A COW'S THOUGHTS

"Good point," said the cow, "Humans are a species not unlike the chewing louse. They produce nothing but more of themselves. They keep busy doin' each other's laundry and mooching off us and the trees."

AFTERTHOUGHT

Fortunately for humans, cows are illiterate.

Dogs

ON APPRENTICE STOCK DOGS

Every fall when I go out to work the cows, the neighbors all show up to help. They come in a big 4 wheel drive pickup, a deer guard on the front, mud and snows all around, a couple of spare tires tied to the stockracks and a handyman jack wired in the back of that hummer rattlin' like a beer can in a fifty gallon drum. In the back of every one of those pickups is at least one good dog, and two pups! All them dogs jump out and commence to fight with one another for two hours. You spend the rest of the day kickin' 'em out from under your feet or chasin' 'em out of the gate.

But you can't say nothin', oh no! You can't criticize another man's dog!

AFTERTHOUGHT
Bax, havin' you and your dog help is like havin' two good men not show up! - Unknown

ON OLD DOGS

I suggested we give ol' Rookie a flea bath. Tink said no. He was afraid the ol' dog would be lonesome. He said Rookie was packin' his own peanut gallery. We watched him walk out to the road and visit with a Doberman female. They sniffed and I saw his tail wag a little and a silly grin slide across his ol' gray muzzle. I said, "Look at that! He's still got a fire in the furnace!"

Tink glanced at his longtime canine pardner and said, "Don't get yer hopes up. I think ol' Rookie's just havin' a flashback."

 **AFTERTHOUGHT**
Dogs and old men thrive on monotony.

ON DOG SAFETY

I interviewed several dogs about the proposed law that would require them to be totally enclosed or securely cross-tethered. The cowdogs were 100% against it. They said, "How would you feel if the government made it a law that humans had to wear seatbelts, crash helmets and drive 55 mph?"

I interviewed two bird dogs, who between them had the IQ of a sandhill crane. They had very little to add.

AFTERTHOUGHT
FOR SALE: Good cowdog, $1000. Will consider trade for two $500 barn cats or a high school graduate with no intention of going to vet school.

- Wally's entry in the Novice category at the stockdog trials looked like a cub bear on his first date! He had the attention span of a Bartlett pear.

 He looked at me like a feeble-minded dog who had just messed on the carpet.

- You can say a foolish thing to a dog, and the dog will give you a look that says, "Wow, you're right! I never would've thought of that!" - Dave Barry

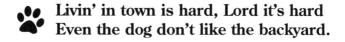

- Nobody loves a kid like a puppy.

Livin' in town is hard, Lord it's hard
Even the dog don't like the backyard.

I've had a run of bad luck but I think it's gonna peak
'Cause my dog that used to bite me got run over just last week!

ON CANINE TIME

Dogs have no sense of time. You can be gone for five minutes or five days and when you come home your dog is so glad to see you! Can you think of a single human being that is that glad to see you? You're gonna run into town, you climb in the pickup but you've got no keys.

You run back in the house...Your dog licks your hand and your spouse says, "I thought you left."

AFTERTHOUGHT
Every day is Saturday to a dog. - Roger Miller

ON BAXTER'S DOG'S OBSERVATIONS AT THE BBQ PARTY - VERBATIM!

Bumbling Black mus be a pirromanyak! He stokd the campfhire with enuf wud to bild a hunting loge, then primd it with a galon of gass. He lit it and blu the hud offe his pickup. By dark the blaz had brrned doun to the siz ov a smal apartmnt complx.

I finuly fownd the hors's. Thay were standing arownd on 3 leggs grumulin abot the fier an makin fune of the roppers. Same confursac-hun I'd herd when I past ther wivs.

AFTERTHOUGHT
It's hard to dry yourself on a paper plate.

Workin' Cattle

ON PUSHING CATTLE DOWN A LONG CHUTE

Imagine, if you will, all of you getting down on your hands and knees single file with your barber behind you and your horseshoer in front. Everybody lined up nose to wallet! Every time you back up to breathe some fresh air, somebody jabs you with a Hot Shot! Not a very pleasant thought...

AFTERTHOUGHT

Each livestock species has its own advantages and each is accompanied by their own particular drawbacks. For instance, cattle require more space, swine have a peculiar odor, and it's hard to run a set of chickens on alfalfa stubble with hot wire.

ON ORDER BUYERS' MISTAKES

He looked like a long-haired Jersey! At least he did to me, and there might have been a camel somewhere in his family tree 'cause he'd shed his hair in patches, past the point of no return, sorta like a shaggy carpet that somebody'd tried to burn!

AFTERTHOUGHT

Please buy the ones in the center of the ring and not the ones leanin' against the fence.

THE BRAND INSPECTOR

∧Z   ⅃₂ Ⅎ⁻ ◇△

The brand inspector stops a steer and runs his fingers through the hair, tracing the outline like a blind man rubbin' the wrinkles out of a wet tee shirt. The only thing that could be more difficult than reading brands would be finding a stud in a wall covered with shag carpet while wearing welding gloves.

AFTERTHOUGHT

After seeing my brand, the Bar Double B Flying Rocking A X Slash, I realize, I'll have to register it on the neck, shoulder, rib and hip to make it big enough to keep from blotching. Otherwise, it will look like my cow fell into a flamethrower!

ON AGRICULTURAL FIELDMEN

They exhorted the buyers to rally contorting
like cephalopods
While the crowd stared back, like Buddhas
they sat, reluctantly giving their nods

It's pointless, I'm sure to give'm a break,
'cause they never have any plans
It'd be like giving a watch to a clock to keep
track of the time on its hands

AFTERTHOUGHT

Like the ocean, always in motion, going nowhere.
--Death in Paradise

ON SHEEP CORRALS

If you're lookin' for a hole to send someone you hate, try the sheep corrals at Cat Creek on the rise. It's the only place I've ever stood in mud up to my knees and had the dadgum dust blow in my eyes!

AFTERTHOUGHT

It was one of those cold springs when the windbreak didn't cast a shadow.

ON SHEEPMEN AND COWBOYS

When a sheepman goes in the cow business, or a cowman goes in the sheep business, a mutant is formed. The sheep side of his brain keeps telling him, 'Vote Republican!', go to educational meetings, eat the heel, pay cash.

And the cowboy side of his brain keeps thinking, 'Ya know, I've got all my money in long term CDs, but I'd like something a little less risky . . . I think I'll buy a race horse!"

AFTERTHOUGHT
Wish I could buy him for what he's worth and sell him for what he thinks he's worth.

ON SHEEPMEN

He's wary of folks who dress flashy and offer to
pick up the tab
He'd rather go dutch or go hungry, than to owe
some tin god of the gab.

See I've spent some time around sheepmen
and I've learned this fact about him
If the bugger calls and then raises . . . your
chances of winnin' are slim!

AFTERTHOUGHT
*Lord, I pray that I am right, for Thou knowest I am a
hard man to turn. - Scottish prayer*

ON SEEKING EQUALITY

If we eliminated modern agricultural methods as promoted by animal rights extremists, we would finally achieve what many politicians and the rabid membership of the United Nations have been striving for, for years...equality with the third world.

AFTERTHOUGHT

It takes all kinds. No, it doesn't, we just got 'em all!
-Unknown

ON GRADUATION

"Dad, I've often wondered, does it ever bother you that all your family's educated right

While you, yourself, quit grade school and went to work at home. Does that fact ever keep you up at night?"

"Well, Son, I guess I'd always hoped to do more with my life but I'm thankful for the chances I was given.

All this time while you've been learnin', you've been earnin' a degree and I was only earnin' us a livin'."

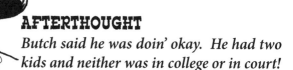

AFTERTHOUGHT
Butch said he was doin' okay. He had two kids and neither was in college or in court!

ON RANCH WOMEN

Ranch women have a lot in common with prisoners in solitary confinement. They are often starved for conversation. This isn't meant to be a reflection on their husband, if they have one, 'cause spending all day talkin' to the dog, his horse, stray cows, passing motorists and itinerant mammals kinda depletes his normally plentiful wit. By the time he comes in for supper all he can do is grunt and fall asleep in the Barcalounger.

AFTERTHOUGHT

On Ranch wives: She offers opinions that seldom sink in 'till time oft as not, proves she was right. But it's dang hard to figger how she could have known? You're not the only one worries at night.

ON FATHERS AND SONS

He quotes his old professors who, I'm
sure ain't touched a plow.
He forgets that twenty years ago
I picked the kind of cow

We should be raisin', but he's so
durn enthusiastic!
And my imagination's lost what's left
of its elastic

I like to think eventually we'll work this whole
thing out
And run this place together, shoot that's
what farming's all about

And we might, if I can just survive
these lengthy conversations
And he don't lose his energy
before I lose my patience!

AFTERTHOUGHT
*Like the acorn said to the tree, "Whattya doin'?" Said
the tree, "Waitin' on you." -Unknown*

ON WORRY

Does a family tryin' to make a livin' on 180 acres work or worry any less than a C.E.O. of General Motors? Does a migrant worker sleep any easier than the Chief Justice of the Supreme Court? Does the editor/owner of a local weekly newspaper put any less effort into his job than the editor of the Boston Globe?

AFTERTHOUGHT

During hard times a rancher said to me, "Yer business of makin' us laugh must be pretty good when times are bad. What are you gonna do when things get better?" Then he thought a second and said, "Never mind, that ain't ever gonna happen!"

There is something admirable about race horse people. They believe in Santa Claus, the tooth fairy, goats, the Easter Bunny, Butazoladin and the next race. They have the optimism of a political campaign manager.

- He rode a Hancock horse with a head like an oil pump.
- The only people that I know who'd ride
  THAT horse, I'd vow
Are too poor to ride a quarter horse and too
  proud to ride a dairy cow.

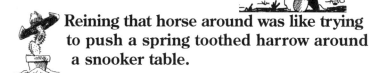

Reining that horse around was like trying to push a spring toothed harrow around a snooker table.

- I'd walk a mile to saddle a horse to go half a mile. - Clyde Ridgeway

- A mule is as good as a horse until you need a horse.

I like living a life where a horse matters.

Rodeos

ON PUNKIN ROLLER RODEOS

White Oaks, New Mexico. The gate on the only bucking chute was made of a six by eight piece of airport landing. Conrad reached to mark out the wild mare whose backbone stuck up like the sail on a marlin. He hung his left spur in a hole in the corrugated metal sheet. He bravely hung on till he was twenty feet long, then lost his grip and dangled, head down from the gate, his hat cutting a furrow in the mud as he swung back and forth like a pendulum.

By the end of the rodeo I looked like a dyin' duck in a thunderstorm. Con's ankle was the size of his head and the chute was in pieces. We were lucky, though. I heard later a feller broke his leg and one of the bulldoggers was never found!

AFTERTHOUGHT

Rodeo is not a hobby. If you want a hobby collect stamps.
- Ty Murray, world champion

ON A GREAT RIDE

When Marvin Garrett nodded his head, no one knew that eight seconds later the Thomas and Mack Arena would be covered with goosebumps. Somewhere in the last two seconds Marvin reached his limit. Everything in his firebox...experience, intuition, talent and training were at full throttle and blowin' blue smoke.

If you'd touched him at that moment it would'a been like layin' your hand on an electric motor. He was hummin'! Marvin had ridden Try Me with all he had left...will, want to, gumption, grit, whatever it is that allows housewives to lift cars off babies and Samsons to pull down temples. Marvin brought down the house!

AFTERTHOUGHT

Ray Hunt is a horse trainer. But that is like saying Tiger Woods is a golfer. I could borrow Tiger's driver and slice one into the parking lot. I could get on Ray's horse and look like a monkey on a sheepdog.

ON AMATEUR BAREBACK RIDING

At the quarter pole of the arena the bareback mare bogged her head, planted her feet and exploded into midair! By the time she lit on all fours again, Jack had both legs on the left side and was laid across her like a roll of carpet! He couldn't get his hand free! All his weight was stickin' out like a wind vane on the starboard side.

After the wreck Russell studied his pardner. Jack's shirt flapped in tatters on his right shoulder. The offside of his head looked like somebody had hit him with a fourteen inch rasp and his arms no longer hung symmetrically. Russell figgered the eyebrow would grow back.

AFTERTHOUGHT

Equistitician - An equine aestitician, one who softens horses hooves by soaking them in a mud hole.

ON THE NIGHT LEO MADE MY POEM COME TRUE

Like Little Joe the Wrangler ridin' ol' Blue Rocket, Leo, my hero, Camarillo glided outta the box on Stick. His loop built from four feet to twelve feet as he fed it. One, Two, Three times he swung. The rope lashed out and he dallied. I looked at the scoreboard. FIVE FLAT! BOTH HOCKS! The crowd went wild... I almost swallered my chew!

AFTERTHOUGHT

I happened to be there at the NFR the night Leo and his partner roped their steer in five seconds flat. It ranked in my mind with John Alden pitonning up Plymouth Rock or Neil Armstrong making angels in the moon dust!

ON CATCHING YOUR DIGIT IN THE DALLY

"When my thumb popped off, it sailed over my horse's head pretty as you please. My good dog jumped up and snagged it in mid air!"

"Great Scott, son," said the doctor, "Whyn't you shoot the dog?"

"Shoot the dog," the cowboy said, "He's the best one we've got!"

AFTERTHOUGHT

When Winston Churchill and Richard Nixon gave the Victory sign, you probably thought the same thing I did...them boys ain't team ropers!

ON BEING BUCKED OFF
IN THE CORRAL

"Well, at least it isn't broken," he said as he wiped his face with his good arm, "Although it might be a smidgen out of place."

That sucker sure did buck hard! I'm glad I was wearin' my hat or I'da punched right through that net wire fence and hung there like a bat!

But I hung on to the neck rein as I spun and ricocheted like someone tied a chicken to a helicopter blade!

AFTERTHOUGHT

When a horse trader says he is "sound as a dollar" he means when you thump him on the belly with yer finger it sounds like an empty propane tank.

ON THE BULL RIDER'S LIMP

When I was a kid we had what we called the 'bull rider's limp.' If you had been entered up the Saturday before, you could develop a limp and make it last all week! When a good lookin' sweetheart asked what happened, you kinda shuffled and shrugged it off. "Got hurt," you'd say.

"How?" she'd ask on cue. "Ridin' bulls," you'd explain nonchalantly.

Images of John Wayne, stoic and brave, filled the air. The dragon slayer injured saving the damsel. The concerned female dabbin' peroxide in the bullet wound creasing your shoulder.

"It's nothin'," you'd say, wincing in pain. If only you had a saber slash across the cheek.

AFTERTHOUGHT

Ol' Hard Luck's head bounced off the back, it sounded like a shot! Like someone threw a bowling ball against a cast iron pot.

There ain't no point in stoppin' now. No reason on this earth. If he's alive, he'll be okay until we reach Ft. Worth.

*And if he's dead as Coley's goat he'll sure be hard to lift
He'll be a dang site easier to move when he gits stiff!*

ON THE RELUCTANT WILD COW MILKERS

"Don't worry," Red assured the other members of the aging Wild Cow Milking team, "Billy is gonna be our roper and he ain't caught anything since the Asian Flu!"

To their consternation, Billy snagged the cow's head and she tumbled. Jerry the mugger started toward her as she rose from the ground like a breaching hippo! Billy's slack was already tangled! Mama cow was goin' 60 when she hit Jerry full in the chest and walked him like a footlog!

When Red rose from the milking position and turned toward the finish line, he stepped on his batwing leg and cartwheeled tush over tea kettle! He spun like a sea turtle on a sidewalk! The precious drops of milk dribbled into the sand.

AFTERTHOUGHT

When asked if I've ever been in a wild cow milkin'. I said, "Never on purpose."

Cowboy Logic

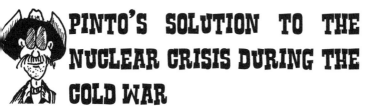

PINTO'S SOLUTION TO THE NUCLEAR CRISIS DURING THE COLD WAR

Attach twenty radio controlled hand grenades to the ten most influential politicians and generals from each side, like rings in their noses. All twenty grenades would be on the same frequency and controlled by the big red button that launches the first missile. Knowing they'd be the first to go might make them re-evaluate their commitment.

Pinto estimated the cost of the new weapons system to be about the same as a 1962 double-wide with a propane hook up.

AFTERTHOUGHT
Like the cow said, "I'm too dumb to stop what I'm doing."

91

ON UNCLE ALBERT'S WAGONS

Uncle Albert put a tarp over the camp wagon and wrapped it with about 60 foot of rope. "Ain't you usin' too much rope?" asked a buckaroo. "Nope, sonny. Every year these new hosses manage to turn the wagon over two or three times before I git'em gentled proper. And this is a whole lot easier than pickin' everything up!"

AFTERTHOUGHT

Free advice is always worth more than advice you have to pay for.

ON PREHISTORIC VEGETARIANS

Some folks would like to believe that cavemen were vegetarians. A little scientific examination and a dose of common sense pokes so many holes in this theory that it leaks like a chicken wire roof. For instance, meat is the exclusive natural source of the essential Vitamin B 12 and the most readily available source of other B vitamins. The iron in red meat is four times more easily absorbed by the body than iron from spinach. Does that sound like coincidence to you?

AFTERTHOUGHT
My idea of a vegetarian meal is a turkey sandwich.

ON THE COWBOY DRESS CODE

The dress code for everyday cowboys ain't
changed since Grandpa was seen
A good pair of boots, yer Sunday hat and yer
newest pair of blue jeans.

Besides, deckin' a cowboy out in street shoes,
a suit and a tie,
Would leave as good an impression
as croutons on a cowpie.

AFTERTHOUGHT
Always wear a tie the color of the main course.

ON CHAUVINISM

I was sitting with a couple when I heard the man remark, "My dear, I think I've seen that dress before." "Yes, you have. I was wearing it the last time we went out. I believe it was two thousand and four." Then she chastised him severely and I'm sure she had a point, and I'll admit her wisdom right up front. But my simple cowboy logic led me down a different path like blind men feeling up the elephant. If women understood our thinkin' they might cut us all some slack and maybe their attitude might soften. When he recognized his spouse's dress, the thought occurred to me, the crazy fool's takin' her out too often!

AFTERTHOUGHT —×—×—×—×—×—×—_{AP}—×—×—
Never build a wire gate tighter than the wife can close, or a bale heavier than the wife can lift.
- *Anonymous (on purpose)*

95

ON MORE COWBOY CHAUVINISM

Most cowboys are chauvinist pigs, which seems sort of pointless because the women they hang out with are not intimidated anyway! These women have never questioned their equality. They may bat their eyelashes, but they look you in the eye when they are doin' it.

AFTERTHOUGHT

It's been said that the Indians really didn't worry about the white man coming into their land until they started bringing their women with them. That meant only one thing, they planned to stay.

On starting camp fires . . . a good Indian always carries a can of gas. - Louie Jannsen

• Most of the Indians I know are cowboys.

If it weren't for the Mexicans, the cowboys and Indians would have been a'foot.

If there are no dogs in Heaven, then when I die I want to go where they went. - Will Rogers

• You don't have to ride Tornado twice.

Dan remarked that the tortillas in Mexico had a more fibrous texture than he was used to. I pointed out that he had eaten his napkin.

ON BUYING A BRED
THOROUGHBRED MARE

She coughed and raised a heave line that would scare an auctioneer. As I started for the pickup he played his final ace. "She's bred to Poo Bah's brother's son, the finest stud to race!"

I held my nose to show him Poo Bah wasn't diddly squat. He blinked and quickly added, "But I don't believe she caught!"

AFTERTHOUGHT
A man with that many horses . . . would you still take his check?

ON COWBOY CURSES

)) May your sheep pay for your cattle operation.

- May the Western Horseman Magazine run the dude's picture instead of yours 'cause he looks more like a cowboy.

)) May you discover the barn cat missing after you've butchered the rabbits.

- May your rope come tight just as the steer drops off a fifty foot embankment.

)) May the choreboy use your good rope to stake the milk cow out in the bar ditch.

- May your blue heeler bitch get settled by a Pekingnese.

)) May the local gossip discover your Jane Fonda workout video.

- May a Wyoming sheepherder offer to buy your best bull to feed to his sheepdogs.

AFTERTHOUGHT

The rules of the range are simple at best should you venture in that habitat.

Don't cuss a man's dog, be good to the cook, and don't mess with a cowboy's hat.

ON SPEAKING AT A
FRIEND'S FUNERAL

Now the preacher is askin' me kindly to say a few words at his death. So I mumble, "He always was steady..." then I pause and take a deep breath. But I'm too choked up to continue, the crowd thinks I've been overcame. But the mason's screwed up his tombstone and I can't remember his name!

AFTERTHOUGHT

A young boy was shaking the preacher's hand on the way out. He noticed pictures of men hanging in the foyer.

"*Who are those men?*" *asked the boy.*

"*They died in the service,*" *answered the preacher, respectfully.*

"*The early service,*" *asked the kid,* "*or the late?*"

ARE YOU A COWBOY?

I like to think I'm good with cows
a pretty fair hand with a horse
But am I a cowboy?
I'm dodgin' the answer, of course.

I've learned to handle the question,
whichever one wants to know it.
I ante up and say that I'm a better
cowboy poet.

AFTERTHOUGHT
My definition of a cowboy is someone who can replace a uterine prolapse in a 1000 pound range cow in a 3 section pasture with nothin' but a horse and a rope.

ON ACE REID

After a tour of all the bars in Kerrville, TX with Ace Reid, at midnight he invited us to come home with him. I asked, "Shouldn't we call Miss Madge and warn her?" "Oh, no," he said, "I drag people like you home all the time! She treats everybody like a Kennedy."

Well, she laid out a platter of scrambled eggs and jalapeño jelly. He told her, "Miss Madge, these boys have lost their wives. They've lost their ranches. Thank goodness they haven't lost their appetite!"

AFTERTHOUGHT

Tom Hall said he'd been married so long they were on their second bottle of Tabasco.

ON ACE REID AGAIN

I was in Hawaii speaking to the state Cattlemen's association. I noticed they had Ace Reid calendars and his cartoons prominently displayed. I asked if they'd ever had him come speak to them. They said no. "Let's call him," I said. I got Ace on the phone.

I said, "Ace, it's Baxter."

He said as he always did, "Well, son, where are you?"

"Hawaii," I answered.

"HI WAH YA!" he exclaimed. "In 1943 I saved the Hawaiian Islands!"

He was a Navy veteran. I told him that the cattlemen over here would love to have him come and give a speech.

"I can't," he said, "If the Japanese ever found out I was there they'd bomb the islands again!"

AFTERTHOUGHT
Ace was pretty tight for an old wire! - Unknown

103

ON ACE REID YET AGAIN

Ace was walking into a little cafe in Johnson City, TX when the screen door swung open and out came the Secret Service followed by President Lyndon Baines Johnson and Lady Bird. LBJ tipped his hat, said, "Howdy, Ace." "Howdy, Mr. President." "Hi Ace." "Howdy Ma'am." Soon as they had departed Ace ran into the men's room and forged President Johnson's signature above the urinal. He raced out and hollered, "Hey, everybody, come take a look in here!"

AFTERTHOUGHT

Anyone can screw up but it takes a pro to make it a memory. --Robin Moore

Farmers

ON COFFEE SHOP PHILOSOPHERS

It is easy to be an expert if you don't have to stay and clean up the mess. Anyone can make recommendations if you don't have to be responsible for the results. College professors, columnists and show ring judges start a lot of things other people have to finish.

AFTERTHOUGHT
*A shrine should be erected in every town's cafe
in honor of the miracles performed there every day*

*"Upon this site each weekday"
would read the simple plaque.
"Six deacons in their seed corn caps
turn rumor into fact!"*

ON CONRAD'S FARMING CAREER

The feller whose disc Conrad had bent while trying to back his new tractor out of the farm sale, came over to him. He opened his wallet and handed Conrad a dollar bill. "Kid," he said, "You take this and buy yourself a can of gas. It'll be the first and last dollar you make farming, but you'll always have enough to get out of town!"

AFTERTHOUGHT
Can't say as I've ever heard a farmer say, "I'm just in the cow business to make enough money to buy the Chevy dealership downtown."

ON FARMERS AND BANKERS

The farmer told the banker that he'd lost all the money that he'd borrowed. The banker chastised him vigorously. The farmer said "Well, it could have been worse."

"Whattaya mean!" said the banker, "Could'a been worse!" Farmer said, "Could have been my money!"

AFTERTHOUGHT

I was chastised by a farmer during hard times, "I heard you on the radio talk show yesterday. You were optimistic about agriculture. Whattaya tryin' to do, ruin everything we've achieved?"

FARMER AND RANCHER

Farmers think a rope is good for towing farm equipment, tying bales down on the flatbed and staking the milk cow out along the highway. A rancher's rope hangs on the saddle and is only used to throw at critters.

AFTERTHOUGHT

The header drives a fairly new pickup and trailer with a coordinated paint job. The heeler's still buyin' recaps and the paint job on his trailer matches the primer on his brother's barbecue grill!

ON INVENTIVE FARMERS

I was bamfoozled by a piece of machinery rusting in a farmer's yard recently. I asked him where he got it. He'd built it, he said, displaying his ingenuity, he pointed out that the hydraulic lines came from a junked log splitter, the big blade was half an eight foot culvert, the tracks came from a snow mobile and the cab from a F-14 Phantom jet.

When the chicken wire and furnace filters were in the full extended position, it looked like a farm trade show that had been bombed!

"Are you finished with it yet?" I asked.

"Not quite," he said.

"What is it?" I asked.

He adjusted his welders goggles and answered, "That's the part I haven't finished."

AFTERTHOUGHT

I figger Alexander Graham Bell had to be a grain farmer. If not, then how did he find the time to invent the telephone?

ON THE LAND

The strength of Iowegians is in the earth beneath their feet. That don't mean much to a stockbroker on the third floor of a high rise in Des Moines, but to a farmer...it's everything.

AFTERTHOUGHT

Our strength lies not in our commonalities but in our differences and our ability to coexist.

ON CALIFORNIA FARMERS

The steer had escaped from the feedlot and wandered into the neighboring vineyard. J.W. saddled up and went after him. Depending on how you look at it, he got lucky. He roped the steer!

The filly he was riding applied the brakes and both critters catapulted into the grapes! They were separated by three rows of neatly pruned, four-foot tall grapevines that faded into infinity. The good nylon rope churned through the brittle grapevines like a chainsaw! The trio thundered down the rows, leaving a trail of abused merlot.

AFTERTHOUGHT

The California farmer is possessed of mystique
The rest of us sodbusters hold in awe and find unique
But the California farmer, when you turn up all the lights
Ain't nothin' but an Okie with a loan and water rights!

ON FARMERS AND SALESMEN

Everything you try to sell me
just adds to my expenses!
It's hard enough to keep'er
runnin' smooth between the fences.

Can't you see yer takin' up my time,
I've got to go and feed.
So say good by and leave me...what you think
I'm gonna need.

AFTERTHOUGHT

Safe and improved, it gently removes a $5 bill from your hand!

ON IRRIGATING

Irrigation is an art form like welding or running a chain saw. They learn each field like the back of their hand.

AFTERTHOUGHT

Don said he was in the Co-op the other day when his neighbor's hired man came in. Don asked him if they'd had any rain out their way. "Sí, some. But I had other plans for weekend so I put two more inches in the rain gauge. The boss gave me the day off!"

ON THE DARK SIDE OF FARMING

• Never cull a roan cow.

• Never assume a cattle guard will stop anything but an intoxicated bicyclist.

• Never put anything you need on the north side of the shed in the winter.

• Always let the wife drive the rig that is being pulled.

• Remember, the public will support agriculture until the last tractor is repossessed or until the price of food goes up, whichever comes first.

• I met a man today whose dream it is to own a backhoe. I need to invest in him.

ON MACHINERY

Carnivorous chain saws, flammable hydraulic lines, sneaky breaker boxes, metric bolts, cannibalistic weed eaters, malevolent milk lines, and burnt-out parking brakes lie in wait for the unsuspecting cowboy. If you have to plug it in or fill it with gas, I treat it like a biting dog. My personal credo concerning mechanical technology is, "If it doesn't bleed, I can't fix it."

AFTERTHOUGHT

The secret of life is knowing how to take a fall.

ON THE RIGHT TRUCK

I had a Ford and a Chevy pickup. Both of them were '69's. I bought'em both used. It was a lot easier to work on the Ford, which was a great advantage. The Chevy was a little more crowded under the hood, but I never had to work on it anyhow, it just kept runnin'. So I don't know which was the better truck?

AFTERTHOUGHT

I like a pickup that looks like a truck
and not like a tropical fish,
Or a two-ton poodle with running lights
or mutant frog on a leash.

Weather

ON MARCH RAINS

The March rain up north is not a gentle, life giving shower from Heaven to be savored and sniffed. It's more like the angels hosing out their hog confinement shed.

If March was a person it would be an old man; cracked and weathered and cantankerous. Occasionally bearable but bent on maintaining his reputation for orneryness. The kind that won't turn up his hearing aid or zip his fly.

AFTERTHOUGHT

When the sun comes out tomorrow
and sparkles all around
Off pools and puddles standin' like
big diamonds on the ground

I'll remember feast and famine,
but when it comes to rain
Ya take the feast when offered,
if ya live out on the plain.

ON HOPIN' FOR RAIN

There's a fingernail moon hangin' low in the sky. The crickets make small talk as he passes by.

A bachelor cloud thin as fog on a mirror crossed over the moon and then disappeared.

He sniffs at the air that's still dry as a bone and takes one more look at the seeds that he's sown.

And he'll be back tomorrow if somethin' don't change, just hangin' on, hopin' and prayin' for rain.

AFTERTHOUGHT

Like the farmer's duck says, "If it don't rain I'll walk."
- Unknown

ON SHOVELING SNOW

Pore ol' Fred was worried about climbing on his roof to shovel off the snow. So he took his rope and tied it to the back bumper of his pickup in the front yard. Looping it around his waist he went up on the roof and over the peak. His wife left for town...in his pickup. Broke both his legs, his pelvis and one wrist.

During recovery he was sitting around the house in a cumbersome body cast. His wife had the habit of filling her cigarette lighter with fluid over the commode. Later that after-ter afternoon ol' Fred creaked his way into the bathroom like a NASA moonwalker. He maneuvered himself into position and lowered himself, cast and all, down on the seat. Ex-hausted, but smugly satisfied with his achieve-ment, he lit a cigarette and dropped the match into the lurking lighter fluid.

It blew him into the tub and broke his other wrist! *- Told to me as true by the Rads.*

AFTERTHOUGHT

Life is tough, and it's really tough when you're stupid.
- Damon Runyon

ON THE AFTERMATH OF A HUGE RANGE FIRE

The horrible fire is over. Ralph's precious tree is a stick. As dead as a steel post. As dead as a dream. Ralph, my heart goes out to you, sir. But I know as sure as the sun comes up tomorrow you have to plant another tree... and soon. Then this winter you can look forward to spring when that little tree will leaf out and start casting a shadow on the ashes of your pain.

AFTERTHOUGHT

God has to be real or we're all just animals.

ON FEEDLOT COWBOYS
IN THE WINTER

There's nothing like freezing sleet to start a feller's day off right. Yer horse has round feet from snow and ice packed in his soles. From the doorhandles down drops of frozen tundra hang off him like Christmas ornaments made of three day old guacamole dip. His hair puffs like an electrocuted cat and his tail looks like the anchor on a tug boat.

You step off to heave the gate open and break through the frozen surface. You sink past the fifth buckle on your overshoe, flailing madly and your horse backs off exactly two rein lengths! When a steer moves across in front of you he rattles like a belly dancer at a Tupperware party.

By ten a.m. your feet and hands are cold as blocks. Your nose has been running like a distemper dog and your moustache feels like a garden rake. The power's been out for an hour and the coffee in the vet shack is the body temperature of a hibernating newt.

AFTERTHOUGHT
His heart is a feather in all kinds of weather singin' his cattle call.

123

ON DRY STRETCHES

One last look at the rain gauge,
the bottom's covered with dust
One last look at the heaven's,
can't see a cloud he can trust.

"Thy will be done," he whispers
with a faith he can't explain
But Lord, his faith would up some
if 'Thy will' included rain.

AFTERTHOUGHT

Farmers and ranchers are students of the sky. They spend a lifetime lookin' for a blue horizon or a black cloud. It brings 'em luck; sometimes good, sometimes bad.

ON ELM TREES

Shade don't come easy on the high plains. It takes a pretty hardy tree to survive. Ya know, it's hard to kill an elm tree. I've even taken to planting them around my place. I kinda admire something that can take everything God and man can throw at them and still keep comin'.

Shade don't come easy on the high plains. It takes a pretty hardy people to survive.

AFTERTHOUGHT

He had a little fever but he said he'd be okay,
too much to do to lay around and stay inside all day.

"Harry, you were up all night.
You've been through a case of Hall's!"
"I can't stay in the house all day,
gosh, what if someone calls!"

He was sittin' in the pickup, asleep there in the seat.
It was idlin' in the driveway. The dog made it complete.

Like he'd just drove up, or maybe
was fixin' to pull out.
Either way he had it covered
in case someone might doubt

his constant perseverance, but his sweetheart only said,
"You can come on in now, darlin', It's safe to go to bed."

ON WORKIN' COWS IN THE COLD

March came in like a lion and left the door open! It's blowed like a banshee for weeks.
I saddle and ride like some kind of robot. She builds up a temper and shrieks.

The constant thrumming that grates on my skin and pulls on my collar and coat
Like a CPR leach that's hooked to my lungs and blowin' its breath down my throat.

My rein hand is stiff as a claw.

AFTERTHOUGHT

It was so cold the coyotes were carrying jumper cables to start jackrabbits!

So cold North Dakota froze to Minnesota and when it thawed and broke off it picked up three new counties and another U.S. congressman!

So cold between Lander and Casper, Wyoming that the wind froze in its tracks and fell flat on the ground. It smashed everything within 168 square miles. Fortunately no one was hurt.

He said, "The wind never blows in Wyoming."
I said, "Mister, where you from?
It'll take the top offa big R.C. or peel an unripened plum!

March is like a biting dog.

The rock decides where the water will go, and the water decides which rock will stay. - sign in Banff National Park.

What country are you from? I'm from the back country.

Of the desert . . . country is close up ugly and far away pretty. --7 year old kid.

The meek will never inherit Arizona.

TRAVEL LOG

The swallows come back to Capistrano, the buzzards come back to Hinkley, and the neighbor's tom cat comes back twice a year.

• In Washington, D.C., Cadillacs and Lincolns speckled the streets like possum feet and guinea eggs at an Oklahoma BBQ.

• We flew into Mexico on a local commuter airline called Aero Mosca.

• Throughout the trip to Mexico I kept hearing a faint tinkling sound like spurs on a hard wood floor. I realized later that it was only the noise made by pesos devaluing in my pocket.

• Traveling on Mexican roads even in broad daylight can raise the hair on a billiard ball.

• We made it to San José del Cabo where I caught nine tuna, two seagulls, the bill of Pedro's hat and Montezuma's revenge.

• Heber City is so beautiful it makes you wonder if Brigham Young went too far.

Politics

ON POLITICS

In the slippery Land of the Forked tongue, in that place where they skate without ice, where forthright men are as uncommon as an enchilada in the Yukon, Washington (Sorry, George) D.C., James Watt did not fit in.

AFTERTHOUGHT

"I doubt that you'll ever be President, son," he said, and I'm sure that he meant it, "But with your attendance record so poor, you might have a chance for the Senate!"

POLITCS, ANTI'S, AND REPORTERS

 Fame is a fleeting thing, as I was saying to my waiters, Dan Quail and John Kerry.

Political ground hogs are coming out like farmers at a free lunch, modestly proclaiming themselves as "America's only hope."

I talked with a black cabbie in Washington, D.C. in September 1984. He had voted for Ronald Reagan in 1980 but was voting Democratic this election. "Why?" I asked. He replied, "Never vote for an incumbent, son. You can't let 'em get a foothold!"

Waiting for the federal government to do something right is like leaving the porch light on for Jimmy Hoffa. --Pat Buttram

Environmental hypochondria

It takes more effort to help your neighbor than it does to talk about helping the world.

It's easy to be green when it isn't personal.

No hope of 20/20 vision if you've got one eye closed.

ON GENEROSITY

You're generous, which I admire,
to wish to give away
The fruits of a farmer's labors
to those who cannot pay.

Then you and I and Farmer Brown
would each be taxed our share
To send our bounty overseas
until our cupboard's bare.

Then we'd acheive your noble goal;
equality, but listen
What good is equal poverty
without a pot to stand on!

AFTERTHOUGHT

*If you can afford to be generous and are not, it marks
you as a small person. That does not include being generous with somebody else's money, that just marks you
as cheap.*

ON CHANGING POLITICALLY INCORRECT NAMES

STRAY DOG: Misdirected wagamorph.

MUSTANG: Adopted equine derivative.

KILLER WHALE: Masked cetacea.

FAT STEER: Ripened ruminant.

GOMER BULL: Frustrated titilator, no, misguided chromosome depositor.

COWBOY: two-legged ungulate overperson.

AFTERTHOUGHT
"Git along little disinfranchised Mobile Nurture Seeker!"

CANIS LATERANS
UNGULATE OVERPERSON CO.

DUST MOTES

 Never treat lunatics like real people.

• No doubt there were some windy lawyers involved in drafting the Constitution but it appears they were constantly outvoted.

• The lawyer's motto: An eye for an eyelash.

• Nouns and verbs make news, adjectives and adverbs make commentary.

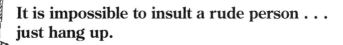 It is impossible to insult a rude person . . . just hang up.

• "Somehow some people have the wacky idea that you'd be better off if the government took more of your money." --George W. Bush

• ABC News said boldly that it, and only it, was "UNIQUELY QUALIFIED to bring you the world." They don't say why or how they are uniquely qualified but, somehow it's hard to put your complete trust in a television network that picked it's call letters just so it could be listed first in the Yellow Pages.

Cowboy
Code

ON SAYING GOOD BYE

Somewhere in the old man's eyes
a memory took ahold.
It fought the ageless undertow
that drains and mocks the old.

I wiped a dribble off his chin,
"Pop, tell me what you see."
"It's all the boys I rode with.
I think they've come for me."

The boss had told me he was old,
had seen a lot of springs.
I bet you if you peeled his bark,
you'd count near eighty rings.

AFTERTHOUGHT
I always nod to a cowboy hat, a real one.

ON WORKIN' FOR WAGES

I've calved a lot of heifers though
    its miserable sometimes,
It's something that I'm good at,
    and it's like she's sorta mine.

She knows I ain't the owner
    but we're not into protocol
She's a cow and I'm a cowboy
    and I guess that says it all.

AFTERTHOUGHT

*At a branding a dude asked me why the ranch crew
wasn't as good at roping as the ones at the rodeo. I had to
explain that the boys from the ranch weren't professional
cowboys, they just did it for a living.*

ON FRIENDS

As I sit here blowing smoke rings from the pipedreams that we've had
I'm wonderin' if I've told him how many times it's made me glad

Just to know he's out there somewhere, like a dollar in my shoe
And how much it would please me if he felt the same way, too

When I add up all my assets, he's one thing I can't appraise,
What's a promise or a handshake or a phone call worth these days?

It's a credit with no limit. It's a debt that never ends
And I'll owe him till forever, 'cause you can't be more than friends.

AFTERTHOUGHT
A friendship is a sum greater than the total of its parts.

ON PERFECTION

That ol' man could sure set a post. Three foot down in the hardest ground, grunt and thud, chink and chime. Bedrock trembled beneath his bar.

Each new whack broke the back of granite old as time. Be easier to move it. The hole, that is. But that wasn't his way of settin' a post.

His ran like a soldier's backbone, straight as a die to the naked eye, perfect...not just close.

AFTERTHOUGHT

In the beginning there was silence, and it was not a word.
--Hank Real Bird

ON ANOTHER GOOD MAN GONE

The last time I called him he was in and out of reality. He was ready, he said. He missed his wife terribly. He became incoherent.

"Call my daughter," he said, "She'll tell ya how I am." I told him I'd rather talk to him if I could.

"I'm not doin' good in these last stages," he said. Then his voice got strong as a bell and he said, "One of these days I'll be lookin' for that ol' black dog up in the white clouds." Then the nurse came on and said he couldn't talk anymore.

He died two days later. A good man. Just one of us who rode good horses, loved a good woman and was true to his friends.

Too bad he can't send me a snapshot from Heaven. 'Course, I guess I don't need one. He already told me what it would be like.

AFTERTHOUGHT
Heaven is not a concept it is a destination. -- All Over But The Shouting by Rick Bragg

• I'd rather have an honest man's word than a crooked man's signature.

• Everywhere I go, ten percent of the people do ninety percent of the work.

• If it takes somebody more than ten minutes to tell you what they do for a livin', they're probably self-employed!

• Too much of anything is almost as bad as not enough of everything.

• The only guy, who can beat the most talented guy, is the one who works the hardest.

• My marketing philosophy is simple . . .everyone's got a twenty.

• A bird in the hand beats two pair.

• VOLUNTEER, from the Greek VOL, meaning to kill oneself, UNTEER, meaning without pay.

• Alvin, the excavator always charged a three percent markup. "Yup," he said, "I just look at a pile of dirt, figger what it will cost to move it and multiply that three times!"

ON MIRACLES

God went out on a limb sending His Son. He took a chance that we'd believe enough in Him to believe in His Son. I guess he expects us to believe in miracles. Maybe that's why most country people are church going Christians; we get to see His miracles on a regular basis.

AFTERTHOUGHT

Unless one assume's a God, any question of life's purpose is meaningless. --Bertrand Russell, atheist

ON FARMERS AND GOD

Because farmers and ranchers have chosen to work directly with God, we get a closer look at life than many folks. We are not insulated from its precarious nature. In return we are exposed to the beautiful sunrise, the smell of rain, the quiet snow and the satisfaction of saving a life now and then.

AFTERTHOUGHT
The big high and lonesome is only God's way of putting man in his place.

- Well, it says it on the dollar, 'In God We Trust'.

- About believing in God . . . It's not always that you do or don't, it's that you can or can't.

- Good and evil have no meaning if there is no God.

- I look up in the night sky in search of God and I see nothing. But I look inside myself and He is there.

- Aunt Effie went to be with Uncle Leonard and God . . . good company.

ON CHRISTMAS TREES

Even the scraggliest Christmas tree
seems to have some dignity
guarding the gifts below

but all of the ones I've seen up close
seem to be smiling and acting the host
to all who say hello

Sometimes I think, if I were a tree
the most that I could hope to be
is one of these wonderful pines

That gets to spend a week with friends
when even a grown-up kid pretends
that all the world is fine.

AFTERTHOUGHT

*So all I want for Christmas is whatever you can leave
But I'd settle for a new wife who would stay through New
Year's Eve.*

Scrambled

WORD PICTURES

Pete peeked into the dark trailer at the sheep. Six big black-headed Suffolk ewes glared back at him malevolently. It was like looking into a cave full of bank examiners!

The motor blew! A big dent appeared in the hood and it sounded like someone had dropped a Caterpiller track into the fan!

With his hard hat pulled down and his cutting goggles in place he looked like a walrus in the Indy 500!

It was then that Lady Luck pulled the table-cloth out from under his dirty dishes. He hit a concrete culvert...head on. It stopped him like a tree trunk stops an arrow.

SIMILES AND METAPHORS

About as obvious as a dead mule in a car trunk.

• Never take a lackey's loyalty for granted. They can turn on you like tuna salad gone bad in the back of the refrigerator.

• The English accent makes one sound cultured. By the time we left England we were beginning to sound like butlers.

• It's spreading like cheap wine on a white tuxedo.

• Fiddles like oil on water, no splash.

• About as organized as a rack of balls after the break.

• I felt like a wino at a Methodist Temperance meeting.

• Slippery as a fish on a Formica table.

METAPHORS AND SIMILES

- Our chartered fishing vessel proved as sea-worthy as a Crescent wrench.

- By the time the boat reached the fishing spot, my face looked like two pearl onions in a creme de menthe.

- Calamari is like deep fried Gorilla cuticles.

- He was so shallow he had no depth perception.

- As useful as pockets in your underwear.

- Windier than a sack full of whistlin' lips.

- A heart big as Al Gore's electric bill.

- Faithful as a birthmark.

- Lightning cracked across the sky like veins on the back of your hand.

- Dancin' like they were sewn together.

- He dove in the water and went to the bottom like a set of car keys.

Don't worry about a thing because nothing is going to be all right.
--Willie Nelson

• Writers don't know anything; they're just impersonating knowledge. --Garrison Keiller

• FDR, when asked how many books and compositions he had written in his life, "Altogether, too many."

• I have never seen a wild thing feel sorry for itself. A small bird will freeze to death and never experience self-pity. -- G.I. Jane movie

• John Milton said, "What hath night to do with sleep?" Of course he would, John Milton was blind.

"Do not assume because I am frivolous that I am shallow, just as I do not assume because you are grave that you are profound." --Rev. Sidney Smith, 19th century British theologian

Honor is something no one can give you and no one can take away. --the movie, *Rob Roy* ©1995

"When you look back, that's when you get caught, that's why I'm still running." --B. Hopkins, on the reason he was still boxing at age 39.

When asked if she was scared about doing a show, Ethel Merman said, "If they could do it, they'd be up here!"

In the beginning there was an empty room . . . with no walls.

Jessica is cliché challenged. Holy chicken? Why did smoke cross the road? --Bro John

You couldn't knock me over with a ten foot pole!

• It was nerve wracking but then I came unwracked.

• Cutaneous staTIStification . . . writing the score on the back of your hand.

• There are three kinds of people, those who can count and those who can't. --internet

• I had my own dressing room with my name on it. Right under the letters M-E-N.

• A barber and a surgeon never say, "Ooops!"

• I'd give my right arm to be ambidextrous.

• Aw, I was just pushing your foot.

• Adios, I'll put an eye out for you.

THE END

BAXTER BLACK

has gained notoriety as a cowboy poet. He has been able to turn this oxymoronic novelty of <u>cowboy</u> and <u>poet</u> into a means of making a living without actually having to go to work!

The stack of books he has written would reach a border collie's eye! He has saturated the media, through his column, radio program, public appearances, public radio and television, and now, RFD TV.

His name rings a bell, even if you don't know exactly why . . . "I'm not sure, but the name is familiar?"

Much poetry written about cowboys celebrates the bravado, romance, and nostalgia of their lives. However, there is a lunatic fringe of cowboy poetry and that's where Baxter has staked his claim.

He is not Ogden Nash, Banjo Paterson, Will Rogers, Mark Twain, Paul McCartney, or Herman Melville. He is his own self, and this book is full of Baxterisms . . . not to be confused with serious writing.

A-10

Second generation Basque-American and full blooded cowboy, Etienne Etcheverry was named after the village in France where his granddad was born.

At around 22 years of age, his friend and rodeo partner would enter them in various rodeos . . . when they'd ask how to spell Etienne, his friend Keith would reply, "I dunno, A dash 10." The name change was official. According to A-10 it has made it much easier to sign his art, checks, wedding papers, divorce papers, ad infinitum.

A-10 is currently teaching art in T or C, NM. He has admitted that nothing is safe from his pen, including but not limited to, mine production reports, oil field water ticket books, bar napkins, tablecloths and bathroom walls.

When asked how he became a cartoonist, A-10 responded, "Well, after living 50 odd years in this dry country, rodeoing, truck driving, potash mining, marriage/divorce, raising kids, teaching school and other life adventures, I had to do something to keep my sanity!"